EARTH-COOL, AND DIRTY

Editor: Zachariah Wells
Cover art: Jaynie Himsl
Book and cover design: Tania Wolk, Third Wolf Studio
Printed and bound in Canada at Friesens, Altona, MB

The publisher gratefully acknowledges the support of Creative Saskatchewan, the Canada Council for the Arts and SK Arts.

creative SASKATCHEWAN   Canada Council for the Arts   Conseil des Arts du Canada   sk arts

Library and Archives Canada Cataloguing in Publication

Title: Earth-cool, and dirty / Jacob Lee Bachinger.
Names: Bachinger, Jacob Lee, author.
Description: Poems.
Identifiers: Canadiana (print) 20210283319 | Canadiana (ebook) 20210283327 | ISBN 9781989274613 (softcover) | ISBN 9781989274620 (PDF)
Classification: LCC PS8603.A299 E27 2021 | DDC C811/.6—dc23

radiant press
Box 33128 Cathedral PO
Regina, SK S4T 7X2
info@radiantpress.ca
www.radiantpress.ca

In this promising first collection,
Bachinger gives us direct poems with a sense of the moment
and the ordinary, that see the landmarks of our lives without embellishment.
The wilderness here is surprisingly close,
it's the nature of every day as we, like some of these creatures,
find ourselves "gambling with oblivion". I found myself re-reading some
favourites for both the pleasure and the thought.

Bruce Rice

The Vivian Poems: Street Photographer Vivian Maier

Coming to us at a time when the words "climate emergency" seem to be everywhere and we're seeing the emergency up close and firsthand, these gorgeously precise, contemplative poems offer not a balm, nor an escape, but a much-needed awakening. Bachinger's intense engagements with Thoreau and Heraclitus are personal and expansive; his Su Tung-p'o poems are exquisite. Sonically alive, metaphorically fresh and wonderfully tight, the poems in *Earth-cool, and Dirty* take us deep into place, relationships, and the nature of desire. I will be thinking about this book for a long time.

Brenda Schmidt

Culverts Beneath the Narrow Road

Jacob L. Bachinger's poems are full of careful observation of the natural world, of people. There are elegies for disappeared grosbeaks, a discarded plastic bag, and the weeds that take over the yard of an abandoned house. But there is also music and reverence and belonging. Like the poet-governor in his eponymous poem, Bachinger's words lead ever homeward.

Monica Kidd

Chance Encounters with Wild Animals

"True poems, as Jacob Bachinger says in his homage to imagist William Carlos Williams, " release the heart." And having read and re-read this excellent book, my heart is transported. Bachinger is, himself, an accomplished imagist, an acute observer, and one is sharply aware of that from the rich blast of sensory detail in the book's title piece. *Earth-cool, and Dirty* brings alive the simple spud in someone else's hands. Some of the stunning imagery that follows is also reserved for hands: his dreaming son's " sleep-softened fingers./ They feel like blossoms." ; and his retired farmer grandfather's work-worn paws, " brown and rusty...like his idle hand tools." I urge you to give yourself over to this true poet and allow his hands to liberate you."

Roger Bell

Candy Cigarettes: A Small Town Memoir

for Shannon

JACOB LEE BACHINGER

EARTH-COOL, AND DIRTY

radiant press

One: The Depths

1 Earth-cool, and Dirty

Two: The Weeds That Run Amok

3 Map of the World
4 Morning
5 Slow Life
6 Pileated Woodpecker
7 Desire
8 Constellations
9 Grief
10 The First Snowfall
11 Ghost Stories
12 The Snow Tells Its Story
13 The Nature of Every Day Is One and the Same
14 Morning (II)

Three: The Garden That Got Away

16 Poems
17 To Su Tung-p'o: Poet-Governor (1037-1101)
18 For Thoreau
19 The End of Nature
20 When Birds Attack
21 Breathless
22 Hand-Tools
23 Little Italy
24 Apples
25 Backyard
26 April Twilight
27 At the Rapids
28 To Heraclitus: Nature Loves to Hide
29 Buteo
30 Audubon
32 Immortal by the River

Four: The Preservation Of The World

34 To Heraclitus: One Cannot Step Twice into the Same River
35 My Son Asleep, Age 4
36 Grandpa: Post-Pastoral
37 Empty Hands
38 Autumn Marsh
39 Ad Larem
40 Loss
41 In Wildness
42 Black-Capped Chickadee
43 Snowmageddon
44 Wisconsin Regained

Five: Wild Clusters Of Inedible Fruit

46 For Dr. Williams
47 Yardwork in November
48 Birch Trees
49 In Preparation
50 Dogberry Season
51 The Green Man for Dinner
52 As Mushrooms
53 The River
54 Où sont les neiges d'antan?
55 Funeral

Six: The Grace

57 Promise

58 *Notes*
59 *Acknowledgements*

ONE

THE DEPTHS

Earth-cool, and Dirty

Dig them with a spade and let them be
spud-dumb, earth-cool, and dirty.
Let them give you grit: black sickles
wedged under the quick of your nails.

Dump them in a basement bin, the depths
where you've cellared apples, home-brew,
the hand-tools you keep handy
for jobs put off until tomorrow.

One winter afternoon, preparing
the Sunday roast, you grope into the moist
and musty corner of the cold closet
where you find them, pale

tendrils dangling from puckered eyes.
And they are uglier, more vital,
than you'd dreamt, cool and round,
earth-dumb in your cupped hands.

TWO

THE WEEDS THAT RUN AMOK

Map of the World

The poem in your hands
might hold it all, as the wind

holds all, lifting
dead leaves and discarded wrappers.

The poem
might offer a map

of the world unscrolled, as when
walking down the street

I found a woman sobbing on her front step,
her face in her hands.

Looking up, she saw me
on the sidewalk, watching.

Not knowing what to say, I walked
away. I was much younger

then. What did I know of sorrow?
Twenty years

have passed and I still can't decide:
did she continue to weep

or, interrupted,
did she stop?

The world has been like this
for as long as anyone can recall.

Now look beyond your hands:
these landmarks are everywhere.

Morning

As a fish
returns
to the river,

so the knife
swims
into your hand:

easy
as a summer morning,
your blood

threading
through the water,
                    the water

whirling
in a stainless, white
basin.

Slow Life

Train the eye to catch
not what's novel, but what remains
the same.

The sag of the neighbour's fence,
sagging like faded pyjamas on some stick-thin body
for years.

Paint peeling from the old man's eaves
and the bony oak in his yard across the way
with those clinging rust-brown leaves.

The street and sidewalk
flat and grey between your homes.

Train the eye to catch
that which marks time, the rhythm
of our world, which is slow and only accelerates
in scattered bursts:

the weeds
that run amok in the old man's yard
when he finally dies,
when his house doesn't sell.

Pileated Woodpecker

Unlikely candidate
for any kind
of accomplishment. A foolish

vessel: neck a frail stem
supporting the flower, the bloody
red crest.

The mumbling,
the hammering, and then
the laughter.

            And yet this un-
balanced
insistence works

the wood: holes, grooves
carved. The tree
carefully fluted,

salient in the soft
light filtered by the forest's
green lens.

Desire

All through winter, wanting
spring. In the arms of your lover, craving
another. Known by many

names and needs: nostalgia, for mother,
her frail voice on the phone;
avarice, for cold coins to clutch;

obsession, for perfection,
washing your hands again, again,
again. Hounds track a scent; daisies seek the sun;

salmon wreck themselves
on a river's rocky ladder. A lack, a lacuna
in the midst of our lives,

at the core of our love: returning
to your father's grave,
certain you won't find him there.

Constellations

Birds scatter, my
neighbour's windows

slate-black in
late afternoon

light, a plastic bag
snapping on a branch

beyond reach, this
memory: my

father, dying,
the end

close,
bare-

foot in summer
grass, gazing

into the night, trying
to learn

the constellations.

Grief

arrives
and it is small: chipped rims
of cups and saucers, scratches

marring the maple table
once Grandma's pride,
grosbeaks fluttering at the feeder—

they came once and never returned.
In all its little dress rehearsals,
grief

is a practice
in this world of forgotten birthdays
and broken windows.

The First Snowfall

The sky will be featureless
and ominous. Birds wheeling overhead

will soon pass. White snow, black trees,
parked cars—the birds, gone—silence

all around you. But not within you.
Watching, you catch yourself thinking

of something else. Some nagging
urge: a cup of coffee, a cigarette,

some small vice, some small comfort.
Something warm. Something easy.

Ghost Stories

> *"shadows of rain moved on far windows"*
> *Ray Bradbury*

Sunlight on a bare wall, bare floor.
Laundry on the line.

Sunday morning liquor store. Church-
bells. Storm clouds building

over the railyard. Toys tucked away
in cardboard boxes. Freighters in the harbour

under grey skies. Garden tools in the rain.
A barn and field at twilight. Library windows

lit on a summer evening. An empty
hall. Footsteps.

The Snow Tells Its Story

The snow tells its story and tells it
slant across all
it touches: ditches, branches, sidewalks,

fast-filling crevices we did not know
were there, telling
its story of a blessing so white

it is a cold curse, falling
to the grey church,
editing the book of its masonry—

tough, grainy flakes changing
every chapter and verse.

The Nature of Every Day Is One and the Same

after Heraclitus

The sun clambers skyward
in its standard miraculous fashion,

and we wake from the labour
of perilous dreams.

Then each of us (sun included)
goes through the motions.

Even if you cannot step twice
into the same river,

nothing is new under the sun.
And yet

    there are days set
    apart—

        the fall
        of Troy,

        Buddha
        under Bodhi,

        the birth
        of my son.

The next morning,
mother and child asleep,

I drank coffee in the cafeteria
then went to the chapel.

Summer light
poured through the window.

The chaplain was kind;
he kept his distance.

Thankful, I prayed.
That, too, was new.

Morning (II)

Before anyone awakens,
the house waits for me

to fill it with soft sounds:
kettle steaming, water pouring.

I sit with the house, watching
for the day:

not the day we will
make, but the one that will

be. The day
that breaks cold

with unswept floors,
autumn leaves.

THREE

THE GARDEN THAT GOT AWAY

Poems

I want them to arrive
like old picture postcards
of boys with rakish cigars and foaming steins.

Instead, they come shuffling like tenured profs
who've been teaching too long,
who rarely have to explain themselves.

They are humourless, but charitable—
like most forms of charity
they tend to fail. The worst of it:

they grasp after epiphanies.
Does anyone need another epiphany?
This one here is guilty, too, I fear.

And yet more than decoration,
they are the artifacts of an old magic, an old cunning
in which words *make*, words *happen.*

When the mountainside hermit
executes the perfect brushstroke and the paint is
crow, flapping erratically from the page.

To Su Tung-p'o:
Poet-Governor (1037–1101)

After long years I have learned
there is a proper use for every tool,
like a window: how to watch
the rain or moon from a window while drinking
a glass of wine.

•

You were exiled,
spending days care-worn, governing outposts;
spending nights with brush, scroll, and
a glass of wine,

which gives the welcome impression
of going home. Far from home myself,
I'm always sure to have in hand
a glass of wine.

•

The mind is a weedy field.
There's no chance of clearing it,
so why even try? Instead raise
a glass of wine.

One day I'll get it right. Things will be
proper: the window, the weedy mind,
all my words leading homeward.

Till then,
a glass of wine.

For Thoreau

Among the ferns, the moss, practicing economy, frugality,
part pioneer, part pastoral aesthete, building your cabin with a borrowed axe,
wanting nothing yet enjoying Emerson's largesse—how easy
to become blinded by the trees in your forest and believe
that the sojourner from Concord, opting for life in the woods,
is telling us that nature is *out there*,
a place to visit, a gallery or museum, when we have need
of a little self-improvement.

But that's the first mistake, isn't it?

It's not just out there but *in here, too*: tangle of the forest,
tangle of the mind, rabbits in the roots, darting, chewing, fighting, fucking
(you wouldn't confess the last one, but we both know it's so),
and when I yank off my boots and sink barefoot into the bog,
captain of my own cranberry party, I sink into myself as well.
And the berries taste that much sweeter, that much more sour.

The End of Nature

for Bill McKibben

Soon we will be everywhere. The end
of nature, everything

touched by the human: heated,
polluted. Nothing left

alone. And yet
even in my own backyard

the tree, whose name escapes me,
stands splayed against the sky,

a dancer caught in music
beyond my range.

We must not doubt it,
our crisis grows—but

the rock in my hand,
gathered from my garden,

is strange to me as my own skull.
Something at the core

is always
withheld, even as we hold it in the palms

of our hands. Even the palms
of our hands.

When Birds Attack

Heed the signs. One attack during nesting season is to be expected. More than a few is cause for concern. Keep spare lumber for boarding up windows. Do not assume songbirds will fail because so many have died against your windowpanes. They will find larger birds. Keep a fire burning. Fire matters more than your gun, which will prove useless. Obey all instructions from authorities. Goggles will do little good. Wear heavy leather or rubber gloves while shielding your eyes. Clean gauze bandages and warm, soapy water are indispensable. If your house is flooded with sparrows, use blankets, brooms, tennis rackets. Retreating to the lawn will leave you exposed. Most birds are diurnal, but night attacks are not unknown. Beware of owls. During a lull in the onslaught, you may leave your home, but go directly to your car. Sexual relations might help ease tension during periods of heavy bird aggression.
It is safe to tell children, "Everything will be all right." Many birds are migratory. By late autumn the severity and frequency of attacks will decline. Pianos, iPods, pots and pans—devices that obscure outside noise—are recommended. The rustling of wings, claws, beaks outside doors, windows, rooftops, and ceilings, is the worst part of the experience. One survivor notes, "It sounds so senseless. So wordless and meaningless."

Breathless

Chipmunk flickers
there—
        there—
                there, on hind legs
scanning the rocks, then
back on all fours
nosing through moss.
You see where it is, not how it got
there: cinematic,
                    chipmunk moves
in jump
        cuts,
always on the edge of something vast
and alarming—a world of hawks, cats, cars.

A bit like Jean Seberg
in Goddard's *Breathless*: wide-eyed,
adorable,

                in jump

            cuts,

                        the slight, sudden critter
on the curb, on the lip
of slate-grey street—small, jeopardized, wide-
                                                    eyed,
gambling
with oblivion.

Hand-Tools

This took me years to learn
because my father despised his job:
all men love their work,

even those who despise their jobs.
A man is trained to use his tools
until the tools become the man.

I can still see my grandfather's hands
long after he'd sold the farm:
brown and rusty,

they rested in his lap, like
the hand-tools he kept in the basement,
tucked away, idle in their chest.

Little Italy

The old porch-sitting women,
their eyes empty of expression,
their rosebushes swollen.

Apples

An old woman owned this house
and she loved the garden—
the garden that got away on her.
In early spring, we moved in.

Busy, we let the garden
fend for itself. We unpacked, painted,
the snow melted, the rain fell.
All summer the garden kept

surprising us, sending us
flowers from tangled, weedy patches.
There was an apple tree, hacked back
till just one twiggy finger

poked from the ground.
Crooked and knobby, an old
woman's finger, the bone
grown around the wedding band

so it can't be removed though
she's been widowed decades.
In October we discovered small
fist-like apples, a half dozen,

rusty gold in the warm autumn sun.
We didn't eat the apples,
just let the season drop them.
Later that month, the old woman died.

We never got to know her. The flowers
bloomed the following spring,
in their fierce, dumb fashion, but
we didn't see the small, warm apples again.

Backyard

after Thoreau's "Spring"

As March rains disperse the snow, baring swaths of burlap grass,
we see how the house has been turned wrongside out and the
unwanted, orphaned scraps and trash banished from our rooms
have found space here, sifting into leaf litter by the sagging fence,
disintegrating greyly on Adirondack chairs, easing into earth among
abandoned toys, sleeping by severed headboards and the Pollocked
ladder resting on its side, joining empty garbage pails, hanging
from the washline with winter's forgotten mittens, dangling with a
broken birdless feeder, thatching deeper into the grass undisturbed
through the feculent spring.

April Twilight

last summer's
spent leaves

small voices
cold breeze

At the Rapids

A boy, his father and grandfather
where the river shoots into rapids:

father follows the muscular current
gathering its strength and charging;

grandfather gazes down to the bottom,
where the rage relaxes and pools;

the boy looks on, wondering,
Where does it comes from, where does it go?

To Heraclitus: Nature Loves to Hide

Where mould grows
on bathtub grout. Loves
to hide

in the kitchen sink: monsoon
with a twist
of the taps. With stray

hair and shed skin
in carpet and bedsheets.
In the shed

where rust gnaws the pruning
saw. Loves to hide
in the collapsing

cantaloupe, soft sludge deep
in the crisper.
To hide in

the coffeepot
cooling on the countertop.
In the fireplace,

in flame. In myself,
as my whiskers dull the razor blade,
as my hair goes grey.

Buteo

Patrolling
fields and

barnyards
from the air,

what does
the hawk neglect?

Audubon

Twilight,
the gloaming,
early winter,

a great
blue heron
on the footbridge

above the river,
turning
from the waters

to cast her gaze
at me:
freakish eyes,

which Audubon
loved to paint—
a slender

dinosaur,
primitive, perduring,
ornate.

Muscles curled,
coiled,
wine-stem legs,

bill
a harpoon—
I sense tension:

grace,
anxiety-edged.
Though I am

alone and empty-
handed, she does not
want my

watching.
She knows
the danger.

A tug
from her broad
wings

on the air,
legs held
straight,

she hauls up
over the railing,
over the water,

to leave me
behind, not far, just
far enough,

to ease
into the mud
downriver.

Immortal by the River

after Su Tung-p'o

If, in spite of loneliness, you can live alone,
at least one source of unhappiness
is diminished.

But I often wonder
if drinking alone makes for an alcoholic,
or is it opening bottles? As I can't be sure,
I do both.

Come twilight you will find me
by the river, on the green, grassy bank.
In the falling dew, I drink my fill
then fall asleep.
When I wake—still drunk—I don't bother
trying to find my way back home.
Instead, I listen to the river.

As for regrets, these three persist:
that my body only appears to be mine
and one day it will be taken from me;
that my mind is full of anxious thoughts
and they follow me like an angry swarm;
that my soul hasn't a prayer.

By the river, when the night
is dark, the wind quiet, and the water gentle,
without effort, without striving,
a small boat could drift far from here.

FOUR
THE PRESERVATION OF THE WORLD

To Heraclitus: One Cannot Step Twice into the Same River

Nor can I re-enter my mother's house
and find it the same,
what with the renovations
since my father died.

Nor can I step twice into the same memory
of my father, for even there

panta rhei
all flows

I find that he's becoming
more like me all the time.

In old photos, I barely
know my own face
but I do see my son's,
there where I thought I'd be,

there in what I thought was me.

My Son Asleep, Age 4

Taking the flashlight and storybook
from his hands, I touch
his sleep-softened fingers.
They feel like blossoms.

The springtime will be short,
I know: mine, his, ours together.
This darkened room, our darkened house.
What no one told me,

what I've had to learn for myself:
to love this much is painful.
Not knowing what else to do,
like a dutiful failure,

I set the light and book aside
and pull the comforter to his chin.
Breath quiet, eyes closed,
he dreams beyond my fears.

Grandpa: Post-Pastoral

After selling the farm,
Grandpa bought cartons of tailor-mades
instead of rolling his own. But he still
wore work clothes: green pants, checkered shirts,
now clean and pressed.

Deep in the armchair, he waved the remote,
weeding channels for *The Price is Right,*
The Young and the Restless. Sifting wheat
from chaff, he said, "If I like the girl, I watch the show;
if I don't, I find another." Then he lit a cigarette
and exhaled discreetly,
deflecting attention from himself.

Without a cigarette or the clicker,
his hands were still.
Was he bored without the farm?
Not that he wanted the work, but
he missed it all the same, as a man will.

Empty Hands

bicycle in the backyard,
disappearing under snow

•

birdless red berries,
sagging on the branch

•

wind over the frozen lake,
searching for the water

Autumn Marsh

October
sedge, cat

tails, trees,
red

wing
black

bird
song—not

pretty but
necessary,

a ticking
clock:

time, please,
time.

Ad Larem

You see them in thrift stores, those halfway houses before the museum or dump. Teacups that clicked when set into their saucers; ashtrays with stubbed-out scenes of Banff, Winnipeg, Niagara Falls; card tables with black metal legs that snapped into the lotus position; rotary dial phones like coiled snakes—how they rattled when they rang. Toothpick buckets, ancient breadbins, now-quiet coffee percolators, cut-glass candy bowls once home to antediluvian peppermints and licorice allsorts (candy you were offered but never wanted), and the occasional owl-shaped table lamp presiding over a cascade of Tupperware nearly tumbling from the shelves. You see them and realize that you had nearly forgotten, but who has not forgotten the household gods? As at the ruins of Pompeii, so at the neighbourhood Sally Ann: the dead gods, the statues of the Lares with their horns of plenty; the old faces, the old mantle clocks with their hands stopped, their gears unwound. You stand there longer than intended, holding an old chrome toaster still dusted with a fine sprinkling of breadcrumbs from distant breakfasts, distant mornings.

Loss

    lives with the exiles
in the basement, the attic,
in an unswept corner of the garage

with broken toys you'll never fix,
skis that won't see snow,
empty bottles and Christmas ornaments.

When all is quiet, when your hands are still,
it finds you
in the kitchen with a sinkful of dishes

or the bedroom with your rumpled sheets—
and calls you like a lover,
calls you from the day, calls you

from yourself. It sits there with you,
drinks what you're drinking—if tea, then tea,
if scotch, scotch—

and quietly confirms your fears—
and it's awful, yet comforting
all the same.

Then some minor mercy
arrives: the phone rings or a door slams,
and you recall you need to be somewhere,

and it's gone,
fled like a feral cat.
But now you know where it lives

and how effortlessly it found you.

In Wildness

is the preservation of
the world, so Thoreau

says; indeed, we find
wildness at work and play

all places: bacteria
brewing in my gut, snow

shaken from clouds, a magpie
claiming my eavestrough

for its aerie, impulsive
condomless sex

one sudden afternoon—wherever
we find vitality

and hazard,
ritual and courtesy,

as when the deer and I
step from the path

to give each other
room to pass, both

attuned to the miracle
of our risk.

Black-Capped Chickadee

In the forest
there is none so
small, so brave.

And with the fury
of one so small, so
brave,

            you perch
on my palm,
demanding

all that an out-
stretched hand
promises.

Snowmageddon

The TV weatherman,
though young and kindly,
warns us: our paved ways
will become our enemies.

Snow plummets, pressing down,
as if God's hand moved,
as if God's hand stirred the sky,
as if God decreed this the first of forty.

Who will dig this divine judgement?
I reap the swirlwind. But after a while
I stop, lean on the shovel,
an ancient penitent on his staff,

and listen. I can't see it, can only
hear: a solitary gull calling,
lost, deep in the white wilderness above.
No route back to the ark.

Wisconsin Regained

Consider global cooling. Imagine an earth gearing for another ice age,
the Anthropocene merely a warm episode between freeze-ups.

Ice caps shrug off millennia of silent sleep and stretch. Glaciers gnaw the
edges of mountain passes. Species found only in northern regions migrate
into new territory: musk-oxen browse in our parks and sports fields.
With snow flurries in June, winter tires become the new all-season.
And with killing frosts in July, crops fail.

Christians claim it's God's will. This time they might be right. Scientists
devise climate change protocols, which are shredded when political will
dissolves. Some politicians, standing in parkas before the cameras, deny
there's any difference. The poor suffer most, but even they admit that
suffering is their special fate. The Inuit, however, enjoy a renaissance.

It would be better that way, wouldn't you say? It would be a pleasure to
walk in our yards and gardens, setting a beer can—likely our last—into a
stubborn snowbank and telling ourselves:
It's not my fault. Not my fault.

FIVE

WILD CLUSTERS OF INEDIBLE FRUIT

For Dr. Williams

Sun burns cold.
Sharp wind scatters
trash along the road.
Ambiguous spring

never quite delivers
what is promised.
Houses on my street:
closed doors,

curtained windows.
I doubt I'll ever know
my neighbours. I doubt
I'll ever know myself.

You wrote, I'm told,
on prescription pads,
a medicinal gesture.
Like nitro, poems

release the heart.
That's how they begin:
hastily scrawled,
cramped scraps

of paper yearning
to hold the cold, wind-blown
streets and homes,
as if by hand. And perhaps

to make some sense
of one's own self,
brokenly, one line
followed by another.

That longing:
I suspect it's all
you and I will ever know.
It's not much, but it's ours.

Yardwork in November

Lost leaves,
copper-coloured,
heaped-up across the grass—

remember years ago
when you could burn your leaves?
That smell

gone
like so much else, gone.
I don't doubt it's for the better,

less of a hazard,
but I do miss it—
that heat.

The teeth
of my rake comb the grass,
a thin scalp.

Below:
the hardening earth,
cold like poor Yorick's skull.

Birch Trees

for Francis J. Child

Cool blaze among evergreens,
crooked, spindly pillar,

bone of a lightning bolt
buried upright, burning

nothing. Its skin, Bible paper
thin, tears slowly, in strips.

Beneath: whiter, brighter
until it weathers.

Touch the peeled bark
and remember women

from youth. Withdraw the hand:
your fingers are powdered

pale, pearl-grey. In old ballads,
birch erupt from the graves

of lovers buried abreast.
For regret, shame, desire,

branches twine and tangle
above tombstones and muddy turf,

saintly white by the kirk wall.

In Preparation

for winter, I listen to the old
carols and ballads, to wind
in the spires of bare trees.

I read brittle paperbacks, the classics,
with musty yellow leaves.
I watch the river crust over with ice,

and run a hand on the stream
of a wooden bannister, polished
by the many hands that came before.

Dogberry Season

These are the dogberry days,
doldrums between Remembrance
and Advent, the only offering:

wild clusters of inedible fruit
hanging from the rowan
thick-grown in the cemetery,

scarlet over the graves, a garland
of unappeased hearts scalding
pale sky and dun-yellow grass.

The Green Man for Dinner

Like a marauding raccoon, he tumbles
through your open window, a stream
of fur, feathers, foliage. Not one to arrive
empty-handed, he slaps down

a dead swan and asks, Will you pluck
and cook it? It sounds more like a command.
You don't know how to say no. Yes,
this will be an evening without apologies.

He winks at your wife. Teeth like a birch
thicket, he grins at your daughter.
After he's helped himself to a snootful
of the John Barleycorn, you find him

chatting up your son. He is ravenous,
eats with ambition, fingers roving
over the food. He wants a second helping,
a third. When he laughs, when he yawns,

his breath wafts autumn leaves
and mossy logs. Crouched in a corner,
the dog is both awed and wary.
He leans back, broad as a sunlit field,

and wonders aloud, What's for dessert?
You know you'll need to find something sweet.
You envy the certainty of his appetites,
the wild grace of his words and gestures,

a barn swallow snatching bugs on the wing.
Post-apple pie, he is grateful, even
humble. Fox-nimble, he vaults the fence
and merges back into mystery—to the vacant

lot next door, the woods behind the strip mall,
the ravine at the edge of town.
Or does he follow the river upstream
to the forest that leads God knows where?

As Mushrooms

Her hands grow over my body,
white thighs, white breasts,
growing over my body,
pale and round as mushrooms
spreading in the warm, blue night,
moist soil freckling pale caps.

When we roll apart, moist,
her round thighs, round breasts
rising and falling, we fall
asleep as mushrooms
spreading blue and ghostly,
heads together in dreaming clusters.

The River

Trees on the hill wade into mist;
mist thickens to fog. Soon the hill
is unmoored,

adrift. As the air clears, I find –
with no slight relief – all have returned,
berthed.

When I climb the hill to the look-out,
the woods are silent. Even the crows
are quiet.

And yet what appears still-as-stone is
merely poised, ready to begin
sculling in the stream.

When the fog returns, I too am drawn
downriver – with trees, hill, and crows –
to a place I don't know.

Où sont les neiges d'antan?

All that slips away:
clothes you wore,
old letters—
I no longer remember

the first time I made love,
recall little of that afternoon
and yet I thought I'd never
forget—all

slipping away until
your final slip, but then
there's no you, just
slip itself.

Funeral

Minus the meta-
physics, death is
practical,

commonplace:
holes in socks,
late mornings, late

trains, boots worn
down at the heels. It is
not knowing

what to make
for dinner and trousers
growing thinner

at the knees.
It is orphans, loss
of income,

the belt cinched
tight. It is a problem
and won't be dismissed.

And it is the rain.
And birds in the rain,
singing.

SIX

THE GRACE

Promise

Most of all, you remember
the grace and wonder,
how they swelled in the car
the night you saw wolves

cutting across the blacktop,
shining in your high beams. Years later
they linger: a promise fulfilled,
as if the wolves were your journey's

purpose, not merely a flash
glimpsed along the way.
Where were you going that night?
As always, trying to get home.

Notes

The Heraclitus quotations featured in several poems are taken from Charles H. Kahn's *The Art and Thought of Heraclitus.*

My Su Tung-p'o poems are reimagined versions of the poet's work that I found in Michael McClure's *Scratching the Beat Surface* and Burton Watson's *Su Tung-p'o: Selections from a Sung Dynasty Poet.* Regarding "To Su Tung-p'o," in an interview with Bill Moyers, Gary Snyder spoke of how, over the years, he had come to learn the proper use of certain tools, like a glass of wine. I loved the idea of the tool-ness of wine, but I gave the sentiment to Su Tung-p'o, who would have undoubtedly agreed with it.

Audubon I'm not sure that Audubon actually loved the great blue heron's freakish eyes as I claim in the poem, yet I imagine that he must have loved painting them.

Dogberry Season The dogberry goes by different names. In some places it is known as the rowan, but it is most commonly called the mountain ash.

The End of Nature This poem emerges from Bill McKibben's book of the same title.

Ghost Stories The Ray Bradbury quotation is taken from his novel *Something Wicked This Way Comes.*

In Wildness My starting point is one of Thoreau's most famous statements: "in Wildness is the preservation of the World." The line is found in the essay "Walking." It's fascinating that Thoreau doesn't write "wilderness" but "wildness."

"Où sont les neiges d'antan?": This poem takes its title from the chorus of Villon's "*Ballade des dames du temps jadis.*" It translates as "where are the snows of yesteryear?"

When Birds Attack Likely this doesn't need mentioning, but I will just the same. Without Du Maurier's story "The Birds" and Hitchcock's film of the story, this poem would never have been written.

Wisconsin Regained My title references the Wisconsin glaciation. The poem began as a question, What if the earth were cooling instead? My satirical answer—in line with Frost's "Fire and Ice"—is that nothing would be any different.

Acknowledgements

A first book takes many years to write and needs considerable help along the way.

To begin, I want to thank Debra Bell, John Kennedy, and the team at Radiant Press. It's been a wonderful experience working with them. Debra invited me to select my own editor, and I'm pleased that Zachariah Wells was able to work with me. Zach's sharp poetic abilities improved every page of this collection.

I also want to say thank you to several other poets and writers.
As teachers, Don McKay and Lisa Moore offered praise and advice; as writers-in-residence, John Barton and George Murray offered valuable help. My poetry group in St. John's, informally known as "the Sheraton in the trees" (because we met in the atrium of the Sheraton hotel), offered suggestions for a number of the poems included here. I'd like to thank the group's members: Jacqueline Hynes, Lisa McCreary, Katie Vautour, Michelle Porter, Andreae Callanan, and Collin Rob Campbell.
For many years of friendship and encouragement, I owe heartfelt thanks to Roger Bell.

Several funding bodies were generous with me and I appreciate their generosity: the Toronto Arts Council; the Saskatchewan Arts Board; and Newfoundland and Labrador's Department of Tourism, Culture, Arts and Recreation for their Arts and Letters Award.

A number of the poems here were first published in various magazines and journals. These publications were very important to me. In turn, I want to thank *The Malahat Review, Riddle Fence, Prairie Fire Magazine, FreeFall, The Lamp* (Queen's University), *Paragon* (Memorial University), *The Society* (St. Peter's College), and *The Fiddlehead.*

Most of all, I must thank my wife, Shannon McAlorum, who, for over ten years now, has been my first reader, my first editor, and my companion in life. She saw these poems through from start to finish, and I'm grateful for her presence and thoughtfulness in the world we share.

PHOTO CREDIT: SHANNON MCALORUM

Jacob Lee Bachinger lives and works in southern Alberta on the edge of the coulees and the Oldman River. He teaches at the University of Lethbridge and has had his poems featured in Canadian journals such as *The Fiddlehead*, *Prairie Fire*, *Riddle Fence*, and *The Malahat Review* among others. He is currently working on a book about his time in Labrador. Jacob lives in Lethbridge, Alberta.